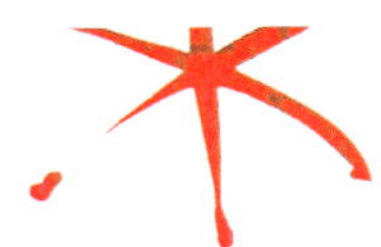

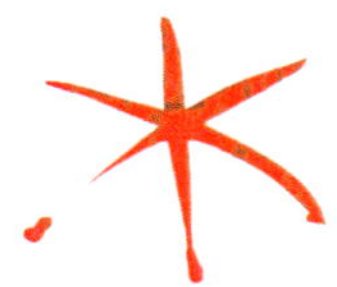

Aster(ix) Journal

www.asterixjournal.com

Editor-in-Chief/Founder
Angie Cruz

Publisher/Founder
Adriana E. Ramírez

Senior Editor
Tanya Shirazi

Managing Editor for *Bending*
Amanda Tien

Aster(ix) Contributing Editors
Rosa Alcalá, Arielle Greenberg, Yona Harvey, Daisy Hernandez, J. A. Howard, Sheila Maldonado, Dawn Lundy Martin, Oindrila Mukherjee, Idra Novey, Emily Raboteau, Nelly Rosario, Zohra Saed, Sun Yung Shin, Jenelle Troxell, Chika Unigwe, Marta Lucía Vargas, Autumn Womack, Elleni Centime Zeleke

Advisory Editors
Ari Ariel, Armando Garcia, Amy Sara Carroll, Norma Cantú, Xochi Candalaria, Jennifer Clement, Edwidge Danticat, Cristina García, Stephanie Elizondo Griest, Andrea Thome, Helena Maria Viramontes

Aster(ix) print issues are usually published twice a year with additional content online. **Aster(ix)** is funded in part by the Dietrich School of Arts and Sciences and the Department of English at University of Pittsburgh.

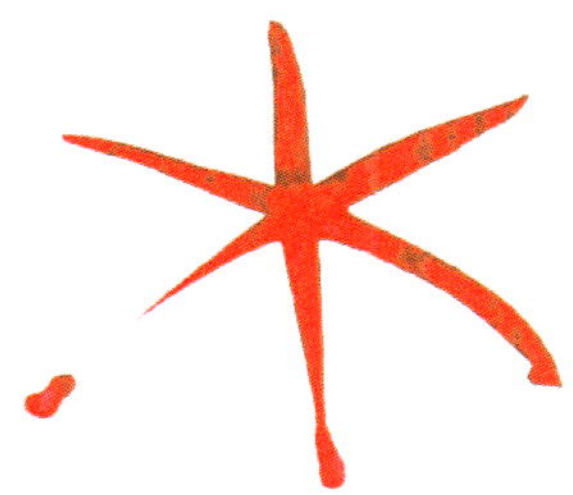

Aster(ix) Journal

presents

Bending

Curated by
Angie Cruz

Drawings by
Laylah Ali

April 2024

BLUE SKETCH PRESS | PITTSBURGH

Published via Blue Sketch Press, Pittsburgh.
www.bluesketchpress.com

Bending.
An Aster(ix) Anthology / Aster(ix) Journal
Edited by Angie Cruz—1st ed.

ISBN (print)   978-1-942547-22-8 (trade paperback)
1-942547-22-8 (ISBN-10)

Cover art by Laylah Ali
Cover Design by Amanda Tien, Laylah Ali, and Little Owl Creative
Interior Layout by Amanda Tien, Laylah Ali, and Little Owl Creative

First Edition: April 2024

Printed in the United States of America
9 8 7 6 5 4 3 2 1

Contents

Drawings by Laylah Ali are interspersed throughout this issue

Introduction by Angie Cruz   9

Call My Mother by Alejandro Varela   12

CAFETERIA TRAVESTI by Julián Delgado Lopera   15

#3 by Victoria Chang   20

Bending Over Backwards by Chinelo Okparanta   23

still here by Nimmi Gowrinathan   26

Green by Caro De Robertis   32

Lookback Window by Patricia Engel   36

A Soul In Descarga by Lilliam Rivera   39

soloist by Courtney Faye Taylor   47

*For years before my tío Junior died,
I wondered if he knew* by Jaquira Díaz   50

Import-Export by Diana Khoi Nguyen   53

For Something Real by Shana L. Redmond   58

Drawing Details   60

Contributor Bios   64

Introduction

Angie Cruz

Reader,

I first came to know Laylah Ali and her work in 2018. We met, and soon after began an exchange where she would text me details of drawings, and I would respond with recordings of unrevised scenes that eventually became a novel. The year 2018 was an incredibly difficult year for me – personally, professionally – but what kept me writing in moments of deep despair was receiving these texts with Laylah's drawings that eventually inspired me to continue writing.

In October 2023, our community felt both despair and rage over global events. Witnessing the unrelentless violence had me asking, What is the role of art and the artist in all of this? If "care is the antidote to violence" as Saidiya Hartman says, then how do we take care of ourselves, of each other and our communities? I was reminded how the creative exchange I did with Laylah felt like a praxis of care.

So, I invited twelve writers into this long conversation I have had with Laylah's work and asked them to respond to twelve drawings from her *Studies* series that she worked on from 2010 to 2013. Some writers chose to respond to specific drawings and others to the entire series.

In the spirit of play and experimentation we curated the issue so the images don't always correspond to the text inviting new connections and considerations. It has been a delight to see how each and every one of the literary contributions have activated the drawings in wild and revelatory ways.

May we all be safe, well and inspired!

With gratitude,

Angie

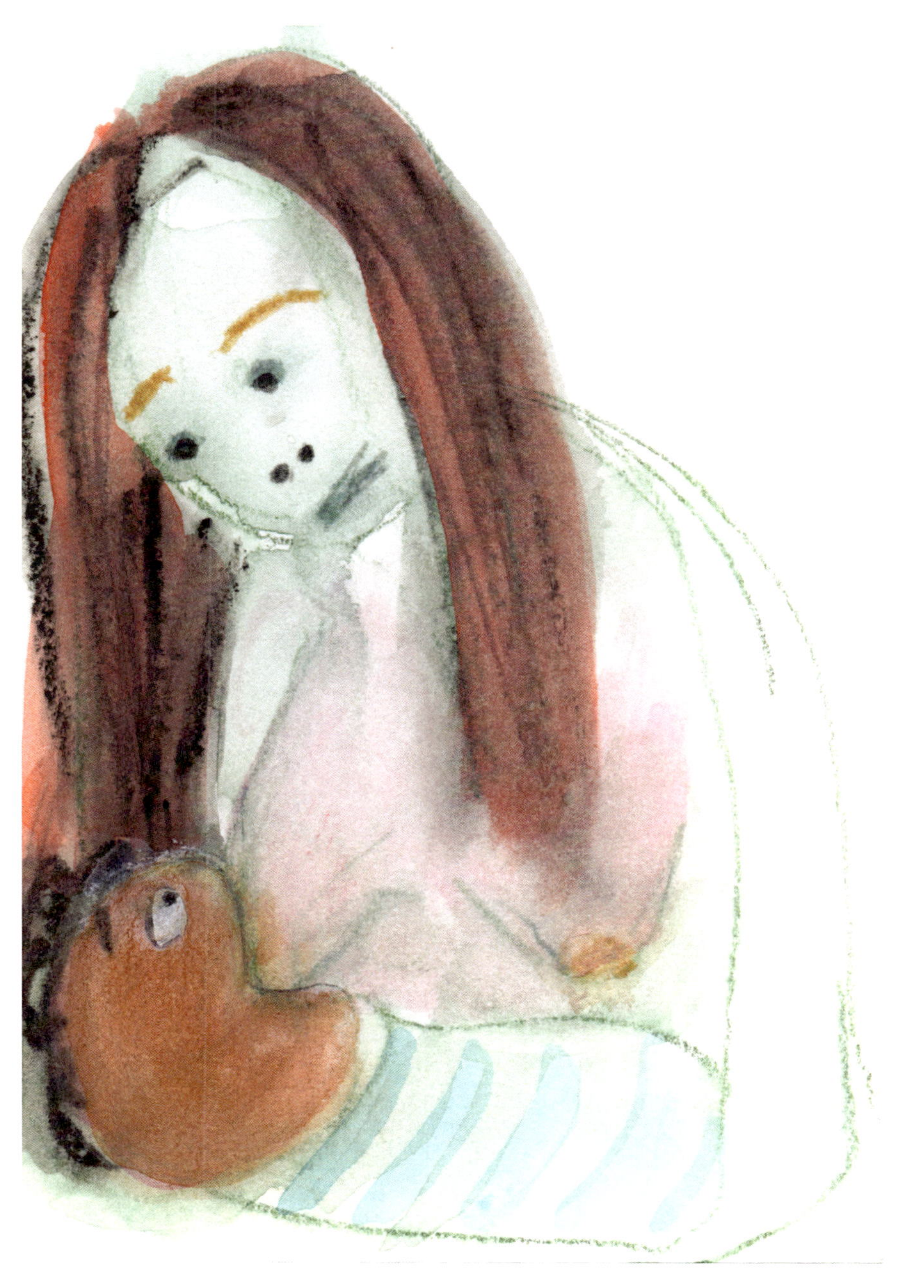

Call My Mother

Alejandro Varela

Sometimes I think I should call my mother less often because she's going to die. She's neither well nor unwell, but statistically speaking, I'm not wrong to worry. If not fewer calls, then shorter ones. Because when she does pass into the immortal realm, I'll be left with a gaping hole in my schedule, and it's this disruption to my routine that will ultimately destabilize me. I'll weather the initial shock, the funeral arrangements, the cremation—my mother insists there's claustrophobia in the afterlife— but I fear the posthumous perambulations: here to there, there to here. That's when it'll occur to me to call her. I'll reach for my phone as I always have, and in those moments, it'll feel as if she's died all over again. I worry about the cumulative effect of her dying every day. What will it do to me?

That's what I was thinking about the other day while I watched the Con Edison guys load ladders onto their truck. God, they must have pensions, I also thought. Pensions are nice. Necessary. Much better than 401ks. Then it occurred to me that my children aren't likely to think of me as a worker, the way I did my parents. My kids are of an economic class and generation that allows them to grow up believing one can be casual and survive—thrive, even. Which may have been why my parents underwent all of it, so that I could one day be casual. And now I am, very. With time to spare. Time to examine the big picture. To summarize, to interpret, to overplan.

I wonder which one of their parents my children will mourn more. It'll probably be me. I'll be the cause of their unexpected free time. My husband is indispensable, but he doesn't seem to need them as much as I do. I try not to show it, but my children know. And in the process of fulfilling my needs, I'll become a part of their walks to and fro, until suddenly, I, too, am a hole in their daily schedules. Or maybe they'll have more time to think but they'll be less thoughtful. I'm also afraid of that. There must be a way to prevent this, no? I wondered about this the other day, instead of calling my mother.

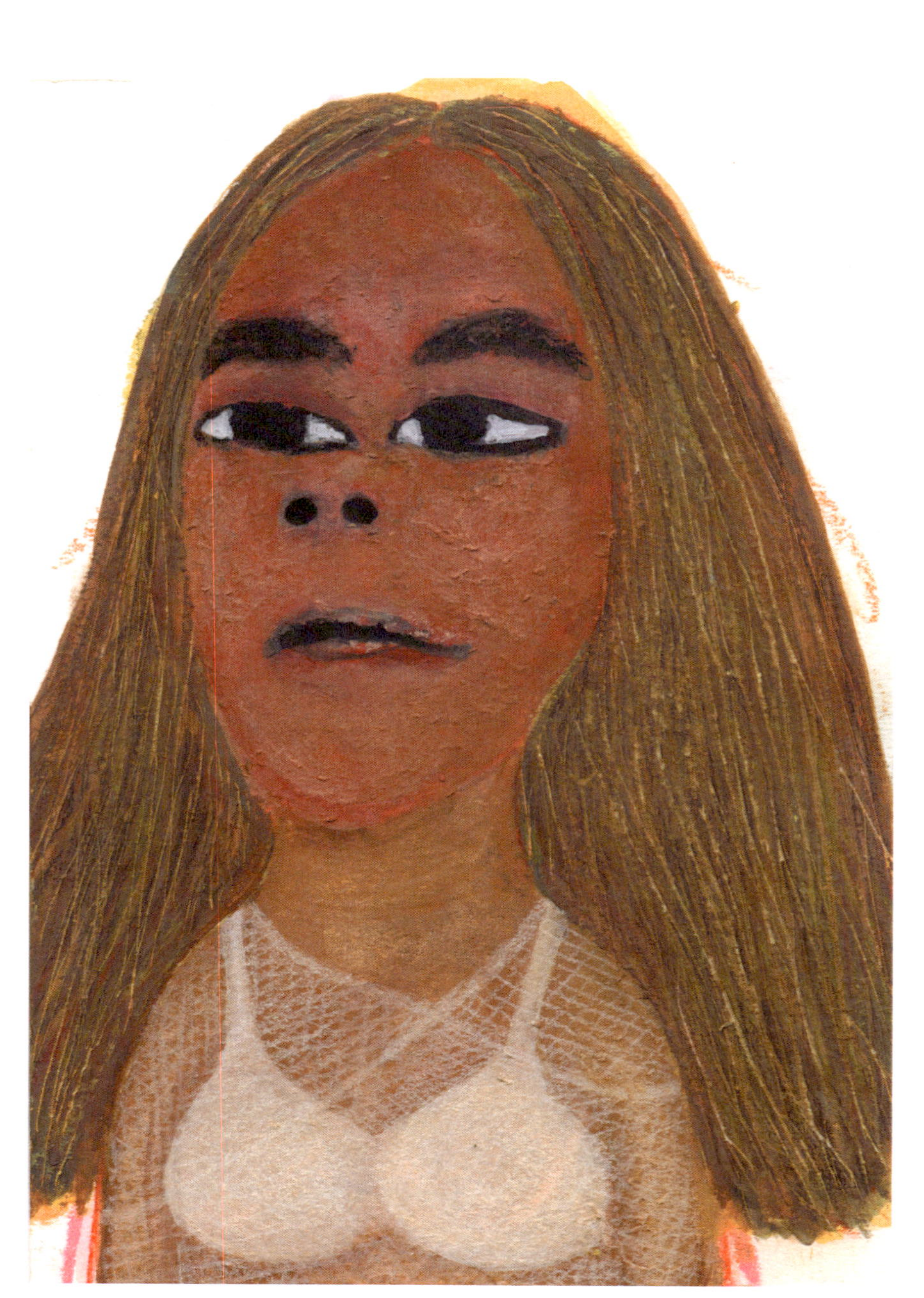

CAFETERIA TRAVESTI

Julián Delgado Lopera

Most people knew her for her iconic arroz con pollo, the raspy voice, the baggies of crystal, her cig dangling from mouth, chopping plátano, setting down paper-plates on the plastic table in her living room for the hungry travestis to eat.

Most people knew Marquesa hugged by a cloud of smoke. They knew the papita churriá carne deshilachá sancochito'e pescao arrocito'e coco juguito'e tamarindo in to-go containers for five bucks: llévelo llévelo for later after working that culito de mundo up and down Polk Street. *Plus*, the Marquesa Combo with an extra ñapa could include one gram of speed to slap life a cachetá limpia and keep the suffering going.

Most people were desperate, hungry, and called her 4-1-5 landline the night before, *Marquesa niña what you cooking tomorrow? Reserve me one plate, two plates. Marquesa niña Ima pay you next week when the GA comes Ima pay you después when God drops all that coin, he owes me.* Sometimes the calls came too late, *niña I'm out of sancocho like I'm out of hope.* Marquesa would say this hugging the phone but still said travesti would show up begging for un poquito of her cooking, for un pedacito of her world. *Marquesa mami give me un pisquito just the tip, just what's stuck to the bottom of the olla.* Everyone wanted to suck her dry of the little she had left, the crumbs of love, the leftovers stuck at the bottom of her own olla, the depth of her bones.

Most people knew the studio apartment on a third floor of a rundown building in the butthole of the Tenderloin, the roaches she stumped with a heel, the bed pushed to the far end corner to make space for Marquesa's Cafetería Travesti. A round plastic table with four chairs, a Virgen del Carmen in the middle. The balada triste of Rocío Durcal coming from the small radio, wrapping the apartment in a blanket of sorrow.
The next day, dozens of travesti eyes crowded that apartment in heels in flats in long-acrylic nails in faux fur coats in thin blunts in *perra where you been?* In *ay Marquesita more carne deshilachá, more jugo'e tamarindo, more love, more story, more of you mamilinda give us all of you,* desparramadas on the plastic chairs, cross-legged on the floor, across Marquesa's bed with the red satin cover and Jesucristo crucified nailed above, cigs on one hand fork in the other chewing on the pollito with rice sometimes breaking into dance and song sometimes a pasito tun tun when the radio spilled a favorite but always, siempre, every travesti oozing her own grief leaking her own cries her own longing her own ven que me muero into Marquesa's Cafetería Travesti.

Everyone came for food and left with a piece of her. Every travesti consumed a chunk of Marquesa, who was the oldest among them, almost 128 human years if you count all the travesti lives she'd lived.

Deep, somewhere inside where no one could see, Marquesa carried Cartagena. She carried the war. She carried her mother's tears wrapped around her like a 50-pound screaming child. The bleeding Sagrado Corazón de Jesús world that pushed her up north to a skyline of fog, pálpitos and tacón alto. What was she but an exiled Caribbean fantasma full of want. What was she but an abandoned ghost.

By the end of the night the girls were spent from all the eating, the shit

talking. By the end of the night, the travesti sadness was a film stuck to every corner of her bedroom. Marquesa took it all in: every spilled travesti heart, every broken soul of her sisters. This tiny piece of world where, for four days out of the week, the tacón alto mafia of the underworld gathered to eat and suck the love out of Marquesa. And how she wanted that. To be the center of a world, to be sucked dry. To be hunger one day, and forgotten the next. To be wiped clean.
At dawn, Marquesa was another animal.

At dawn, the apartment was decorated by stacks of chicken bones piled high on paper-plates in every corner, their own little massacre.

At dawn, it was all a memoria. Puffed brown eyes face covered in vile and saliva glossy skin the color of tierra. What was she but all heart. What was she but a bent over hunger of rage wanting nothing but love.

At dawn, it was the want, the craving inside her to go out into the street, machete in hand and scream, *With all the good people dying every day and God doesn't finish taking my life.*

At dawn, it was her own travesti telenovela.
Starring Marquesa's unreliable heart.

Starring the 3400 miles to an unrecognizable home.
Starring los ojos de su madre.

By the time the sun rose, the knife was in her hand again, the half-ashed cig suspended on her lips as Marquesa hummed a bolero chopping the ripe plátano, messing her damn nails. By the time the sun hit full force the phone rang desesperado bringing the yearning calls of the travestis on the other side, *Marquesa niña save me two plates of pollito and one plate of your heart.*

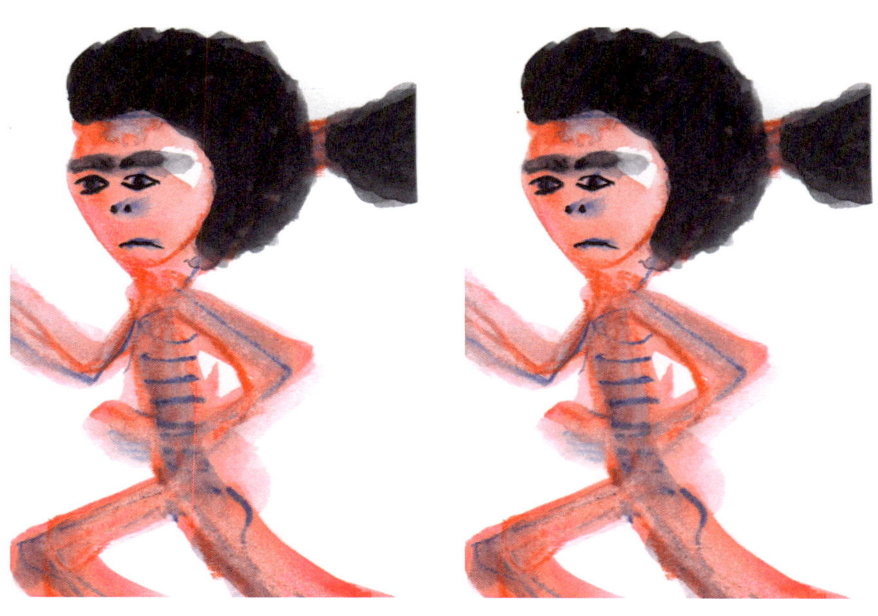

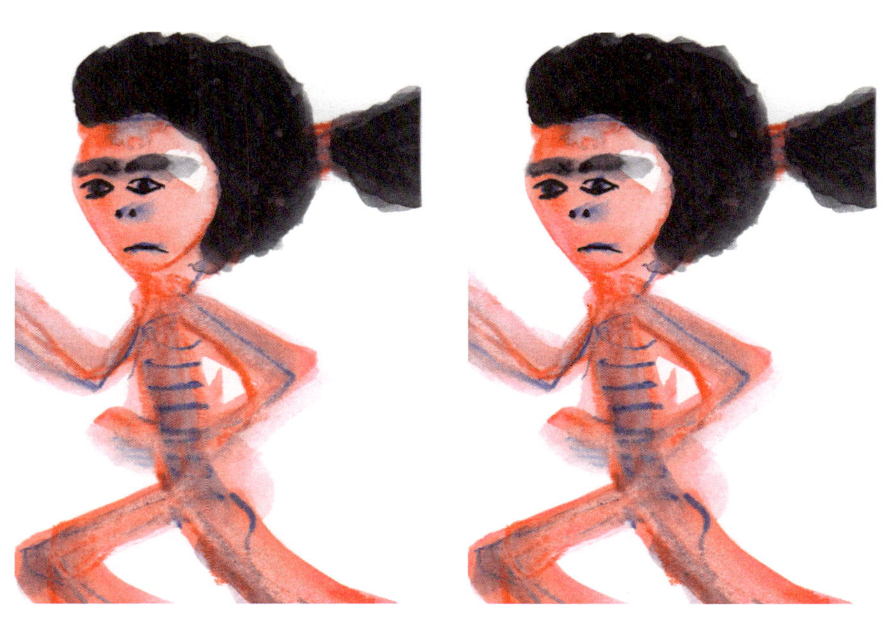

#3

Victoria Chang

I picked the third one because I thought no one would want it. And in not wanting it too, I began to want it. This was my third choice, not the first where the red body or the red hand on the red skirt suffers into the face. Or the second one where one body holds another in time, splitting at the torso so that one body folds down. For me, words come before seeing, to reverse John Berger's assertion. Sometimes, my words come at the same time as seeing. The idea that one is not interior to the other. That the blue lips emerge at the same time as my seeing them, not after, means I have mud within my mouth, not behind it. Some of us only have mouths to be stuffed. Why have a mouth? Is a mouth still a mouth if it cannot speak? Now I am looking at her eyes, two blue dots. Where was she when I was away? If she was not a sight. If she was not being surveyed. Where did her story go in the time I was gone? What if we can't look everywhere at once? But the world demands that we do? Right now, looking down from space, there are small lights from guns, a line of people walking over a mountain like interest. And all the colors of the paintings. I swear by the two blue dots as her nose. The way they dye her eyes blue. The way by themselves, without the rest of the face, they become the universe. There's too much red in the world is what she must be telling us. Her neck red, her breast red, the lines underneath her eyes are red too. As if to say, look, even time is red. The only thing that might not be red is blood. Because after all the killing, what remains is the sky.

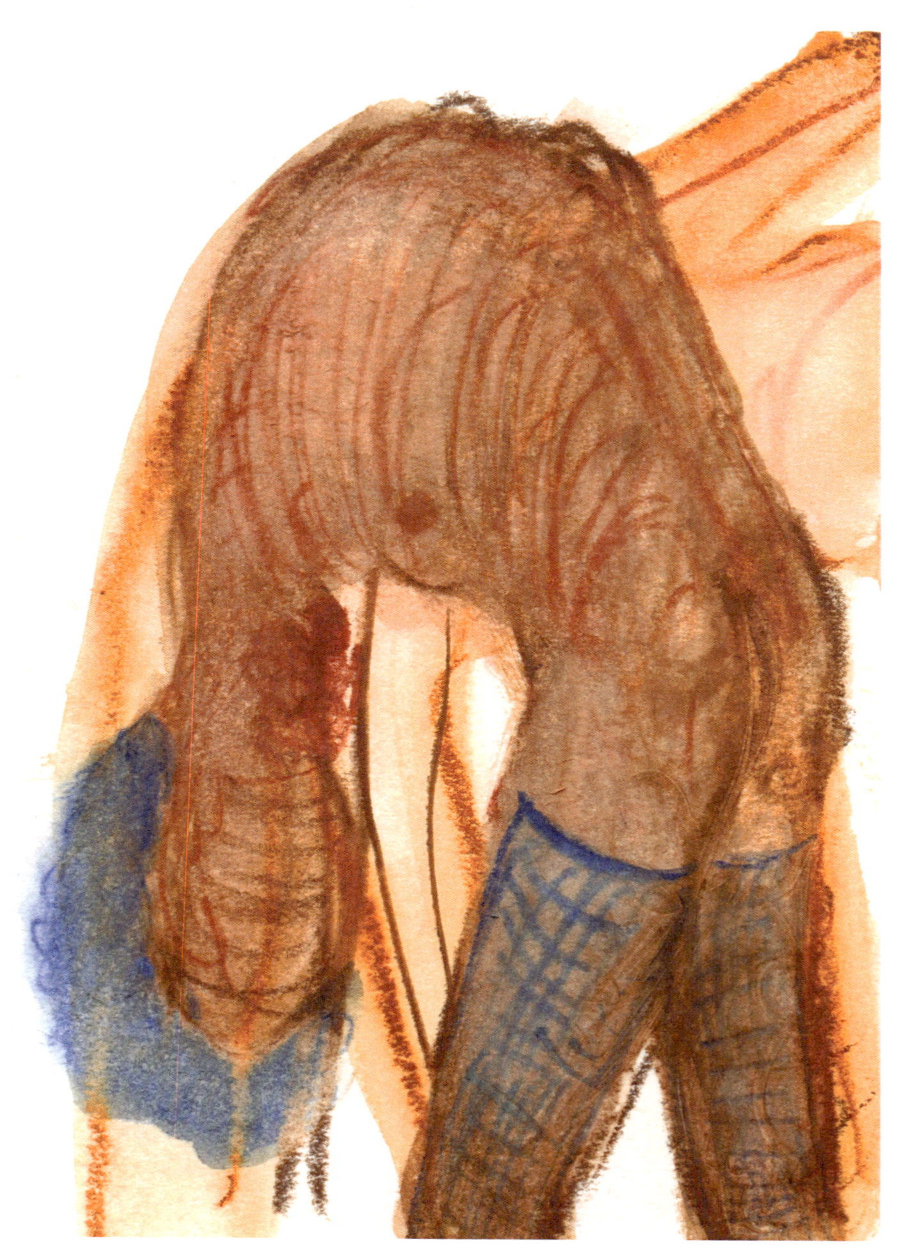

Bending Over Backwards

Chinelo Okparanta

The girl awoke to the sound of crashing rain.

"Why don't you show me what you can do?" the boy asked the girl.

"Yes," the girl replied. Keloid scars stared from her torso like smashed eyes, like old forgotten blood. "Yes, let me show you what I can do."

"Show me," the boy said.

Time passed. Through the window of the dingy ivory-colored box of a room, the orange sun forgot to blaze.

"Show me," the boy said again.

"Can't you see?" asked the girl. "I'm romping and reveling and bending over backwards for you."

The boy saw now, and he liked the romping and the reveling, but he did not like that she was bending over backwards for him. He wanted the gift of the romping and the reveling, but he did not want the receipt of a new keloid scar in his name. He knew that if she bent over backwards for him, she'd give up all of herself to him, and if she gave up all of herself to him, she'd be like all the other girls who'd given up all of themselves to him. He knew that if she bent over backwards for him, she would lose herself to him, and already, he was sitting on a heap of keloid receipts, all those innumerable scars.

"No, no, do not bend over backwards for me," he said. "Not today, not tomorrow, not ever." He saw now that he no longer wanted the girl. He wanted, instead, a girl who would not lose herself to him.

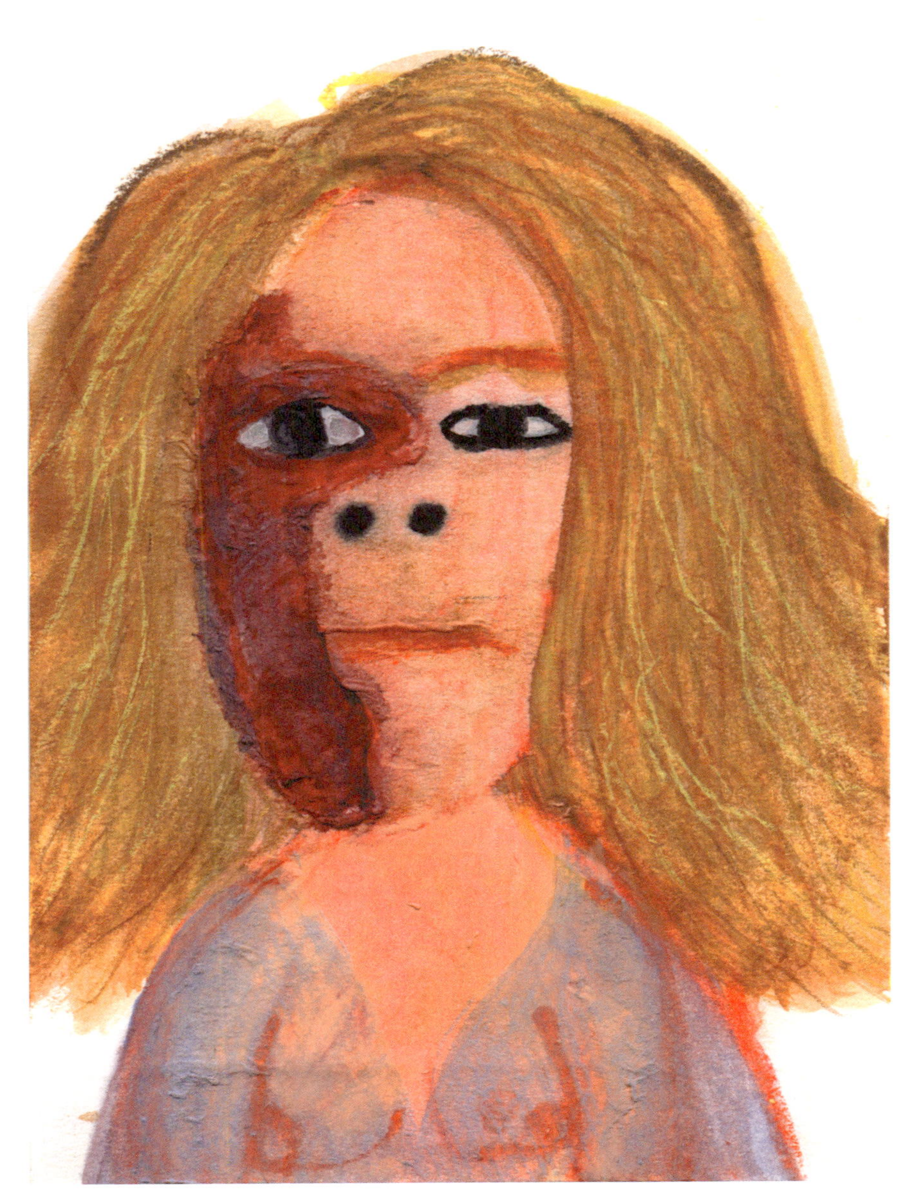

still here

Nimmi Gowrinathan

The side that faces you.

A comadre asks a classroom to sit with the courtroom portrait of a militant nationalist, sketched by Picasso. Djamila Boupache captive in Paris for rebellion in Algeria. Clean, firm, lines distort her features towards orientalism.

She is portrayed as abstract and profiled with clarity.

"History can also be unmade and rewritten, always with various silences and elisions, always with shapes imposed and disfigurements tolerated," Edward Said said. Ears blocked by bias never listen.

Kajol lines swept under an angled eye in a singular motion: inherited muscle memory. Deep inhales stop working for childbirth and fear. Pain sneaks in. Inflamed nostrils garnished at times with a gold ring. The gleam set against skin too dark to be read as the rebellious accessory of boredom in suburbia. Markers of meaning become a menace.
When did a feeling become terminology on trial?

The heat we apply will never quite tame locks out of suspicion. Strands of your colors never fully assimilate with our (ironically) dominant genes. Orange is what happens when white resists brown, a child in America will tell you. We never fully occupy linear language to liberate: a pursed lip prevents shortness of breath.

Too much bodily cover and you are a violent threat, too little and you're vulnerable to it. "We didn't want you here anyways," says a Berlin immigration officer as the scarf falls from your shivering head.

* * *

BENDING

The category to contain us, another comadre in Oaxaca says, has "been affixed so firmly to our faces that it becomes a mask that tries to pass itself off as skin, to eclipse our own self-image."

* * *

This side faces me.

Bloodletting never stays inside the lines. Artistic anxiety itself is shaded, settling differently in the shaking fingers of the dispossessed.

You never realized that the mask of empire was comforting, a lavender-infused soft pillow that blocked the darkness. The enlightened produce well-crafted lines to tether humanity to that which is inherently good. Discourse is the strategically selected filter to cover shadows of atrocity. When it slips, it reveals raw lust: technologies of facial recognition are futile against the technologies of war. In hindsight, it was not enough to recognize the contours of intent when the depths of insatiability were laid bare.

Blood visibly drains from the skin in shock, from the organs after trauma. Rumors amongst the besieged say the enemy (here and there) is experimenting with weapons that render injury invisible. Pain feels the same.

One eye on suffering, theirs and yours. Deep red spreads across the other cheek that never fully turns, only burns under your gaze. Deep breathing does not re-oxygenate old wounds. Blood coagulates around masks that form on the inside. Boundaries, therapists say. These ones never stay secure.

I don't know if the will to resist outlives the longing for death.

We grasp for each other in a blackout, "Are you ok?" The message hovers between you and her, waiting for the double checks to appear.

"I'm still here."

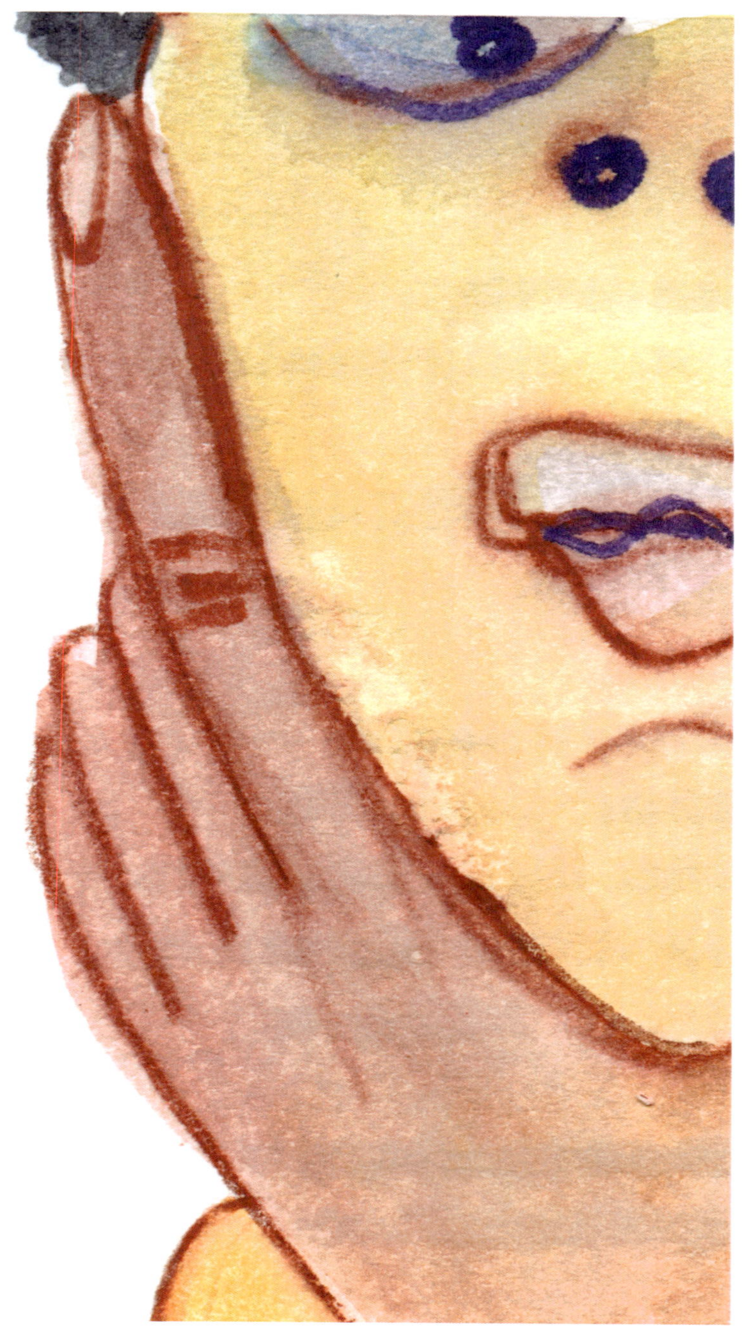

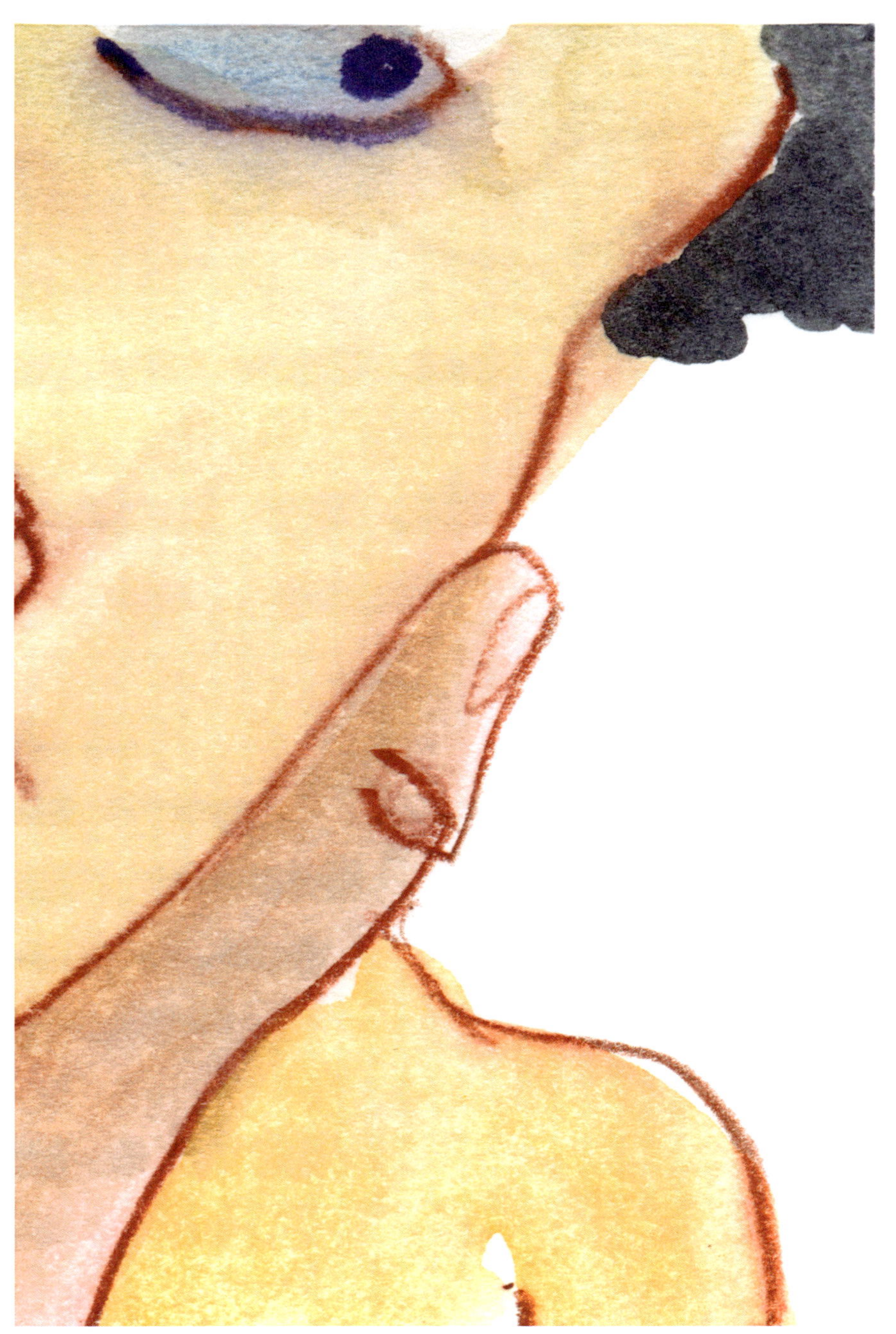

Green

Caro De Robertis

To be bent over like this.

Naked.

Pinned down.

Spread wide. Taken.

Slapped, whipped, called a whore—where did it all come from?

Can it be feminist, she wondered as she spread her thighs, to want this? Can I still be on the side of liberation? All those years of anti-rape work before Me Too, in the peripheries of culture, shouting into the void; all those marches and petitions; all that Taking Back the Night. And now this hunger.

What was this desire?

Why did she beg and beg for it?

How could she feel so safe with this lover who brutalized her with such blazing generosity?

Succumbing.

Surrendering.

Lion was behind her now, fully dressed. Observing. She waited for Lion's next move, for Lion-who-was-Papi's next move, for a signal, for a force that would sweep her off like a leaf in a storm, toward a freedom deeper and wilder than anything she'd previously imagined.

Lion, whom she'd first seen at a leatherdyke social meetup taking place in the same bar where she'd just wrapped up a boring-as-hell first date, thinking maybe it was time to give up on Tinder, what was the point, these draining meetings with strangers when she could be in her own apartment catching up on work. On the way to the bathroom she passed a back room and saw the black-clad women and not-women-but-not-cis-men—trans guys? butches? genderqueers? she wasn't sure but knew better than to assume—laughing and talking and making a raucous music all their own, and there at the center stood a top, in their leather vest, holding their date—could you call them a date?—by the leash. She met the top's eyes. Electricity, immediate and strong. Look away. Rush to the bathroom and out of the bar. Try not to think about that woman (butch? trans man? burning person) with the leash. Try and fail. Find out when the social group meets in that bar again. Show up. Stand outside in the cold wind for too long staring at the neon beer sign in the window, tattooing it to your vision, before you finally go in. Tell yourself you're not looking for any one person, until you find them and your eyes meet again. Lion. It was right there on the name tag, along with pronouns: she/her/he/him/Papi. Of course, she thought, this is the Bay Area, where queers can go by names like Lion if they damn well please (for it wasn't until later that she'd learn about scene names, their hows and whys). As for that last pronoun, it seemed a portal to a thousand things she longed to know.

BENDING

But she'd had to prove herself, that evening and over coffee with Lion the next week. She'd laid all her boundaries and fantasies bare, the way kinksters did, something she'd heard about but never done before with a potential lover, let alone in a bustling hipster café. It made her voice shake and her whole body run hot but she managed to language her wishes and wonderings, her Yeses and Nos and I-Don't-Knows. She had her safewords: red, yellow, green. Once they got to the bedroom, the one she used most was green. To say: keep going. To say: push further. To say: I've plunged into that vast nonverbal zone of sweet obliteration, of annihilated bliss, so I can't shape the words to tell you that I'm okay and I want more.

Twenty years before, in college, in those marches to Take Back the Night, as she and her fellow activists shouted anti-rape slogans at the stars and the shuttered windows of frat houses and administrative buildings, knowing full well that the only listeners who gave a shit were (possibly) the stars, they had trespassed onto manicured lawns, and at the start of the march in the gathering twilight, the grass had still shone green. The strength of their steps and voices had given her the illusion of power, bright and fleeting. She thought of it now as Lion hovered behind her, at the canvas of her bare ass, poised to unleash something new. How, back then, her body had seemed a vessel for something large and thrilling. How she'd longed for the green beneath her feet. How she'd wondered what would happen once the night was taken back—if they ever took it back: what they'd use it for, whether night could be home, could be harnessed as a place to come alive.

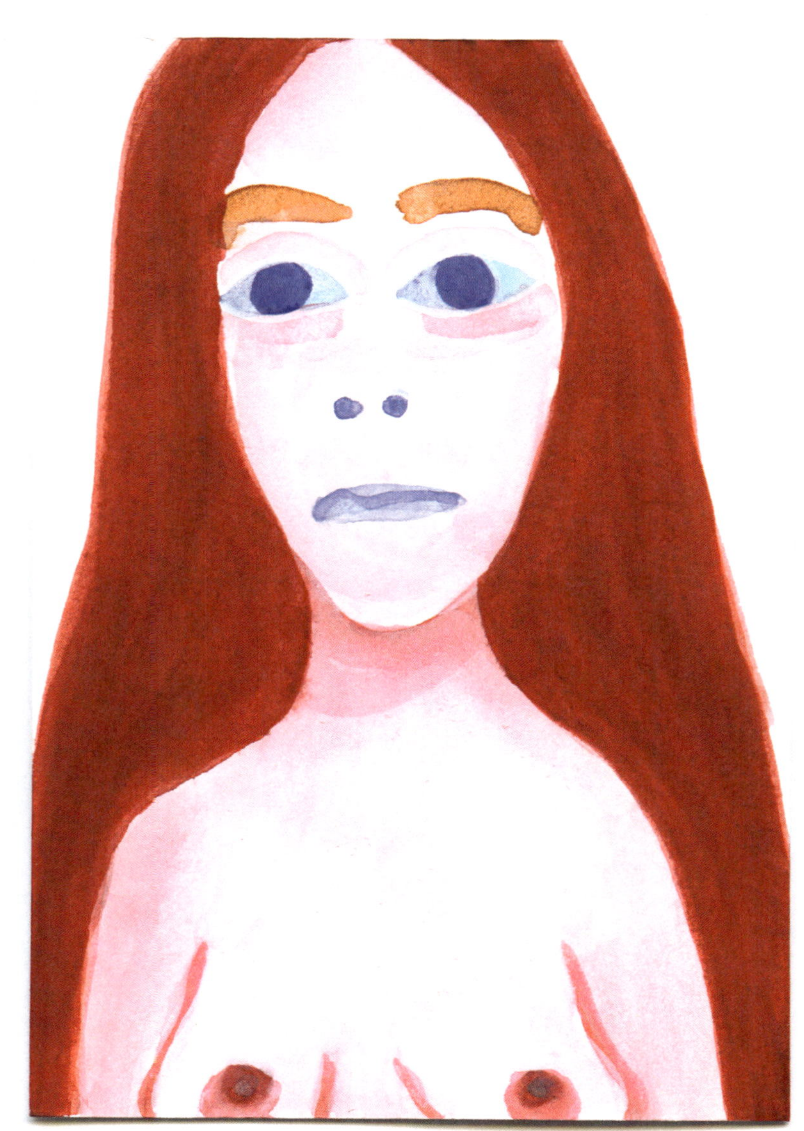

Lookback Window

Patricia Engel

New York

She tells me I am beautiful the same day he says my face disgusts him. She tells me I am brilliant the same day he tells me I am not as smart as I think I am. She tells me I am a loving human being the same day he tells me I am selfish and spiteful. She tells me I am brave the same day he tells me I'm a coward. She tells me I am a survivor, a hero, the same day he tells me I am a viper, damaged, dead. Long ago he made me think possession was union and union is ownership and ownership requires loyalty and loyalty is compliance; that a woman can be claimed like land, a stake driven through her body's soil. Long ago I learned silence is shelter and poison. I spoke in broken sentences to sisters who heard the missing words because they speak the same hushed dialect. There is no endurance without the swell of time, the pressure on the torso, the legs; grief's inertia. They are two people: the he of then, the he of now. But they are the same, demanding submission. Lookback window says the Act, the pursuit of civil relief, a chance to review what memory made unspeakable; symbolic justice is no justice but light burns clear fire when pushed through glass. He stole my face. My original smile. I search for it in old clothing, photos, in portraits that were not hijacked, tainted, sabotaged. She tells me it's because he hates me that he treats me this way the same day he tells me it's because he loves me that he treats me this way. She tells me I can remember if I try hard and I can forget if I try harder. The lawyer wants dates, proof of conversations, those I briefed after the fact. But I told no one, not knowing there is a statute for sorrow, not knowing there is limitation to how long one may legally grieve their own passing. There is no secret diary, no hidden calendar. Court does not mean crime does not mean prison does not mean truth. The lawyer says you cannot attribute memories without witness, conversations without corroboration, you cannot remember certain things and forget others. You cannot summon a ghost to trial. You don't understand, I say. The ghost is me.

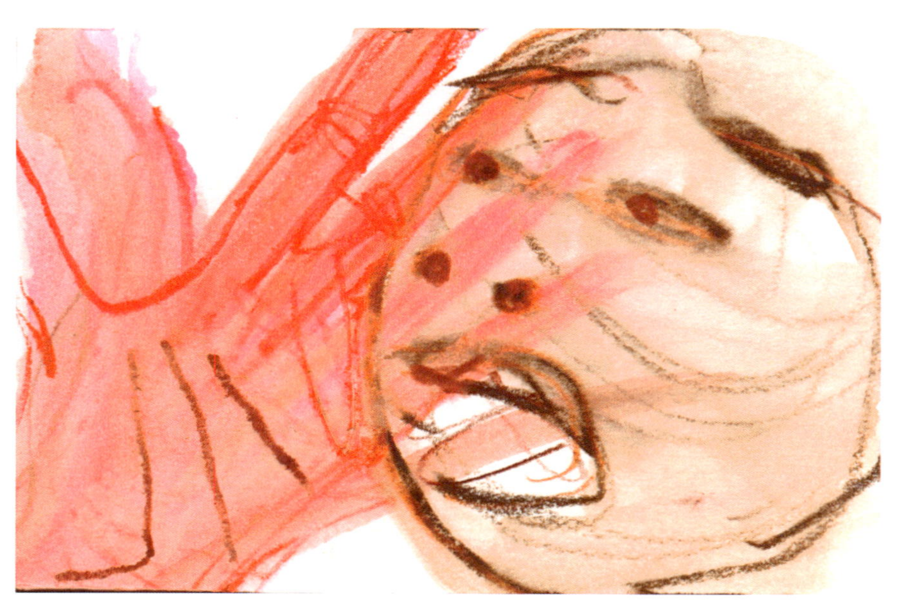

A Soul In Descarga

Lilliam Rivera

Las Chicas del Bx Group Chat
Friday, 6:40pm

Millie: Have you heard from YaYa? She's been
MIA since yesterday

> Lourdes: She prob took another job
> on top of her ten other jobs.
> [Picture of dusty pink stilettos]
> What do you think?

Millie: Oooh, I love that color. how much?

> Lourdes: On sale!

Millie: Check if they have my size but
it has to be wide. I can't do narrow,
thanks to the Colon family. We're
like giants, stomping across rooms
alerting everyone we've arrived

Lourdes: I'll look. you working? anyways,
this bitch trying to tell me how
I've been slacking, coming in late
and shit, being slow with the orders.
you know me. I let that bitch talk
and talk and talk and when she
finally finished that caca like she's
the boss and not just another
heaux stuck in this office like me,
I said all calm,, "I'll do better."
but you know what I wanted to
say is I FUCKING QUIT or
BITCH YOU UGLY or FUCK YOU.

Millie: You need the job.

Lourdes: I need the fucking
job so I can buy shoes

Millie: We all got to play the game.
Do they have my size?

Lourdes: No.

Millie: Do you think she's writing you up?

Lourdes: IDK. Maybe.

Millie: What does IDK mean?

Lourdes: Bitch, tu si eres vieja!

Ask your daughter. LMFAO

Millie: At least I know what LOL means

Lourdes: These would look good on YaYa.
[Picture of black stilettos]
Oye, where is she? She hasn't checked
in since last night. Come in @yarelis

Yarelis: [image of drawing]

Lourdes: Que eso???

Millie: YaYa, what's going on?
Why are you showing us that?

Yarelis: I'm just standing
here in front of this, crying
como una pendeja.

Lourdes: Where are you?

Yarelis: I woke up raw, so I
called in sick. And now I'm
here, at the museum. I don't
even know why.

Millie: What's wrong YaYa?

Yarelis: I feel like I need a
cleansing.

BENDING

Mille: Why???

Yarelis: This painting, it
makes me think of her. How
she'd press her cheek against
the small of my back and
listen to my breathing.

Millie: Oh YaYa, it's coming up,
the anniversary. Isn't it?

Lourdes: Maybe your mother's
sending you a sign.

Yarelis: She'd say, each inhale
 is a gift from god. No se, I
was mad at everyone back
then. What I would do to
have her listening to me
right now.

Lourdes: idk, you finding this painting,
making you think of her. She's trying
to tell you something.

Yarelis: You think she wants
me to finish my Masters?
You think she's disappointed,
like I'm wasting away my
life? Cuz when I look at
these dancers in the painting,
melting to the ground, it's

                    like Mami is looking straight
                    at me, shaking her head.

Millie: What! Disappointed?
All you do is work. You've never
called in sick. Never. Should I
come get you? You're not going to
do anything crazy are you?

                Lourdes: YaYa, you looking at that
                painting all wrong. It's a bendicion.
                Your mami is saying to live.
                Wasn't it Audre Lorde who said,
                what we have to do must
                be done in the now?

Millie: That's right, YaYa, Lourdes is
right. Your mama is saying, live.
Feel. Dance. We know this
because we're your sisters

                Lourdes: [Heart emoji]

Mille: [Crying emoji]

                        Yarelis: [Broken heart emoji]

Millie: Let's meet at Charlies
for R&B night. YaYa, don't stay
in this sorrow. Come out with us.

Lourdes: [Picture of black boots]
Do you want me to get you these?
They have your size, wide. Te lo compro?
YaYa, what's your size?

YaYa?

Las Chicas del Bx Group Chat
Friday, 7:02pm

Millie: YaYa
say something

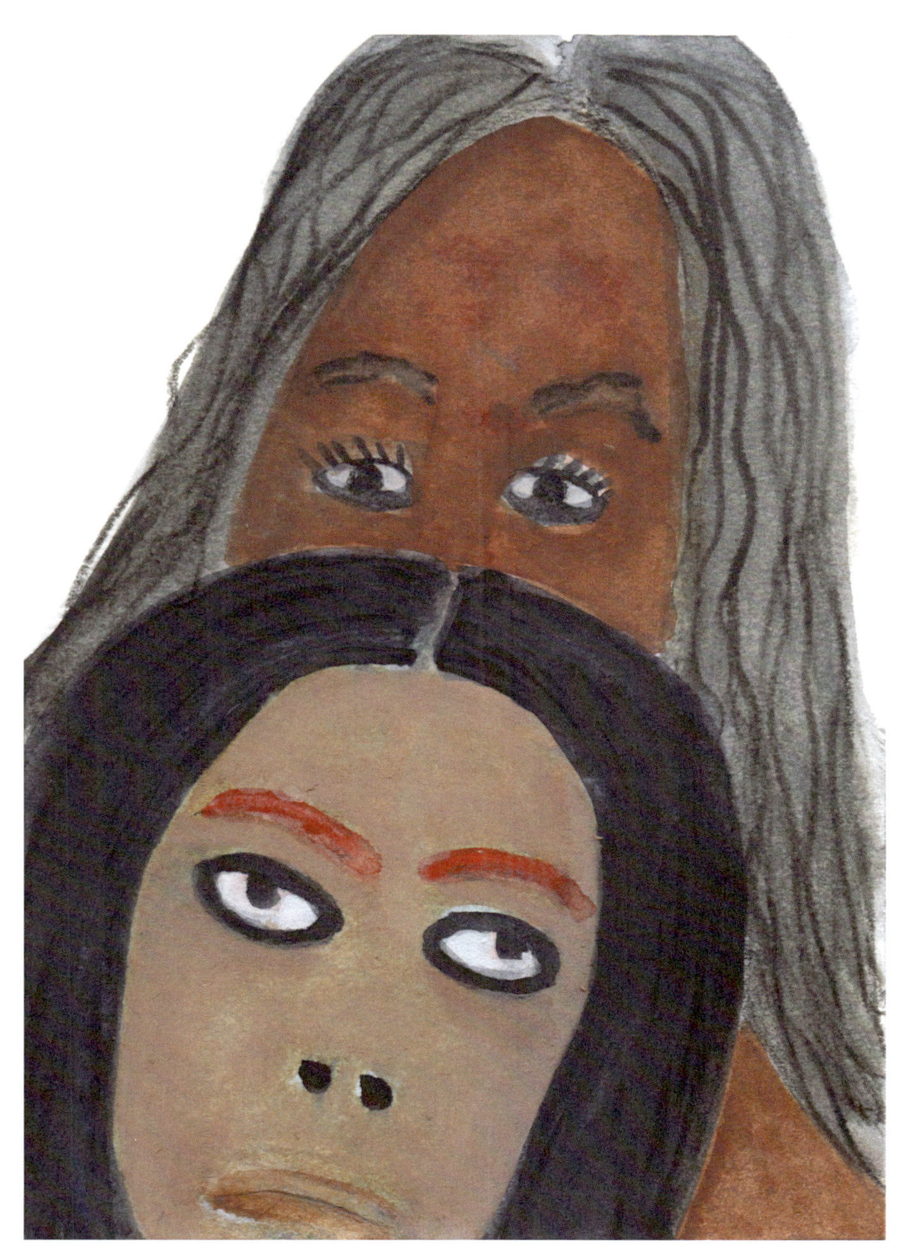

soloist

Courtney Faye Taylor

My aunt was the director of the children's choir and responsible for doling out solos. She assigned me, *I Know It Was The Blood*, a hymn we did monthly at communion. Back then, I retreated whenever I had to hold a mention of crucifixion in my mouth. Singing about bleeding felt unwise to me, like a wish to be brutalized or empty.

We rehearsed for hours, practice often touching the evenings, making me late for *Degrassi*, which began with a recap of the previous episode at the top of the hour. The montage served to remind me who amongst the cast had fallen pregnant, wrong, or ill. Without those segments, it was impossible to tell one character's psychic wounds from the next. Without recap, riskiness is everywhere. Everyone has it.

All week, the hymn repeated in me, even when I wasn't singing it. My head, alive with *blood king, blood cross, blood mumblin', blood tomb*, then soon my sensitivity wandered off completely, refusing to be recalled or bothered. So I was good with bleeding, respecting it as admonition, as the body's means of telling a truth. Bleeding, how the body keeps its contract with honesty.
The morning of my debut, we rose early for a final run-through. Birds exorcized their nervous systems on the sill. The dryer, inhabited by house shoes, mimicked the sound of assault. I sang. But when my aunt slid the lid over the Yamaha keys and ushered me out the house, I admitted I didn't want to sing it anymore. *I'm too afraid to sing it anymore.*

The bulb in my aunt's face, a watt beyond brilliance. That's how beautiful she looked, keeping her contract with honesty. *You're not afraid of singing. You're afraid of your singing being heard. And if you're afraid of someone hearing you, you're just afraid of being alive. Don't you know life comes with singing, speaking, breathing? Don't you know all of it puts you at risk of being heard?*

And I wrestled with this idea for many years, until I made a contract to never wrestle with ideas. Yes, it's impossible to be afraid of singing. My fear is a fear of the lifelong audience, an obvious fear for someone born to witness the risk of being witnessed.

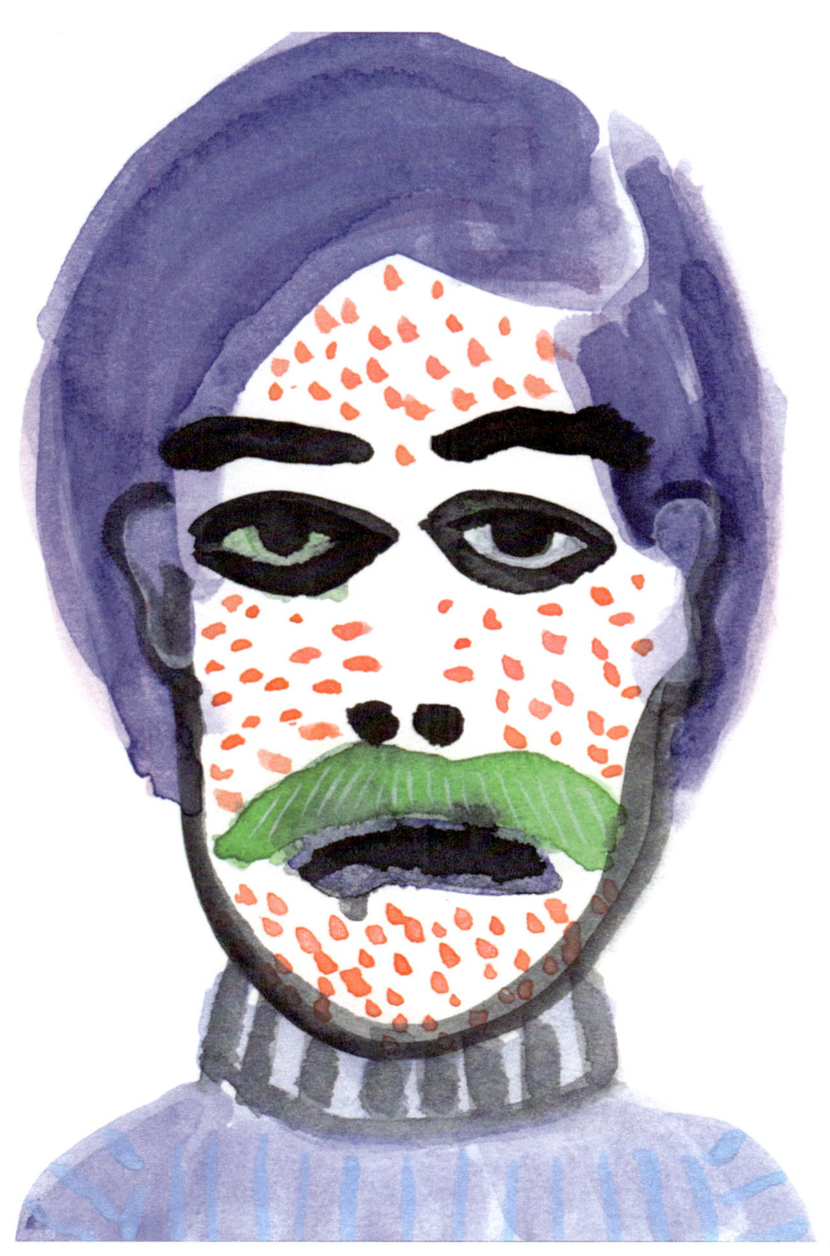

For years before my tío Junior died, I wondered if he knew

Jaquira Díaz

Did he suspect when he watched me shoot hoops in the park? Or when he told me, a million times, to pull up my baggy jeans? Or when he caught me kissing la vecina's daughter when we were both twelve? I was grateful that he'd never told my parents. Never told anyone.

Pero la vecina's daughter? She confessed to her mother when she got caught skipping school. Confessed everything she'd ever done, including all the kissing (it had been more than once), and all the cigarettes we'd stolen from our mothers to smoke behind our building. La vecina told Mami, and together, they confronted us both.

I denied everything. There had been no kissing, no cigarettes, none of that. No way.

My mother turned to la vecina's daughter. "Tell me the truth," she said, her nostrils flaring.

La vecina's daughter got so spooked she cracked. Took back some of what she'd said.

"I made up the thing about the cigarettes. But the kissing, that was real. I swear on Jesucristo."

I wanted to scream! She had a chance to take something back, and she went with *the cigarettes?* And on top of that, she'd used Jesucristo against me! I would not be kissing her again. Ever.

Mami gave me a whooping I will remember until my dying day. Took a skinny belt to the back of my legs, and I cried so much I threw up.

After my tío Junior died, I wondered what it meant that he'd never said anything. I resented what it implied: that I had done something so wrong, so shameful, he took the secret to his grave. Eventually, I realized he'd been protecting me. How he'd been more than my tío—the one person who believed I could do anything, my accomplice, keeper of my secrets.

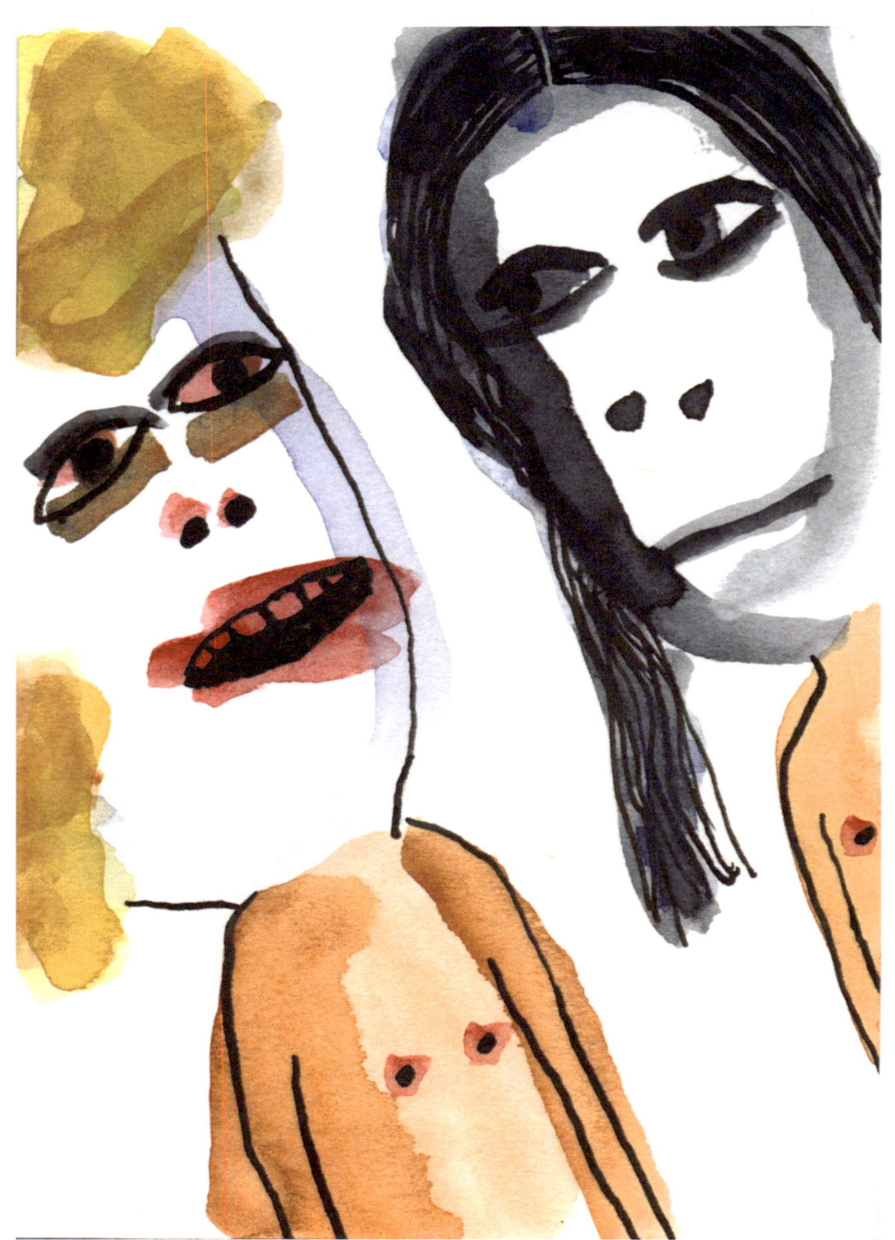

Import-Export

Diana Khoi Nguyen

Two days before she gives birth, the thirty-eight-year-old watches a breastfeeding video from a national health institute, but it's hard to practice without a baby. When she remembers that masturbation is generally a solo activity, she is able to secrete colostrum, an amber bead forming at her nipple.

*

Two nipples like two shower heads with some pores clogged. The thirty-eight-year-old doesn't know which directions milk will squirt, nor when she will stop leaking.

From the bike commutes of her twenties, she knows that black hides wet spots better than any other color.

She reads that the "maternal skeleton is borrowed from during lactation to provide much of the calcium that ends up in breast milk," and wonders about this import-export business.

*

The baby is a by-product of fluid exchange from one parent to another, and calcium flows from one skeleton to another.

Sometimes the zero-year-old unlatches during a feed, and the milk sprays across the zero-year-old's face. Opalescent drops cling to the zero-year-old's eyelashes like dew on the tips of a crabapple tree in October.

*

If she rides her lover's body, she faces away from him, so she doesn't shoot milk into his face.

*

Years earlier, when she nestled in bed with her eight-week old puppy, he had latched onto her nipple and sucked.

*

After years of unrequited sexual longing in a past monogamous relationship, the thirty-eight-year-old discovered that her libido disappeared when she brought the puppy home.

*

Two years before his suicide, the thirty-eight-year-old's younger brother told her that his libido was back.

*

The thirty-eight-year-old's lover told her he found pregnant women to be erotic. But when she was pregnant, his libido mysteriously vanished. The thirty-eight-year-old didn't feel like any of the pregnant women she'd seen or read about. Like a creature undergoing transformation, she was alien to herself, host to another alien inside her.

*

Alien, client, patient. Once she knows she loves her parasite, the thirty-eight-year-old will assign it a different name. Once she's a parent.

*

The thirty-eight-year-old knows what the one-year-old doesn't: that both have moles on their genitalia.

*

When the zero-year-old is a one-year-old, she will point at the mole on her mother's jawline and say, "Mama." She will point at her father's mole and say, "Mama." Sometimes after pointing at her mother, the one-year-old points at herself where there isn't yet a mole, and says, "Mama."

*

The thirty-eight-year-old doesn't recognize herself when a photograph is taken of the right side of her face. She knows the face is hers, like how she knows an avatar is her in a dream. But she doesn't feel that her face is actually hers.

*

The one-year-old isn't mine, the thirty-eight-year-old thinks, but belongs to the one-year-old herself.

When the one-year-old grows up, will she recognize her features in her parents' faces?

The thirty-eight-year-old couldn't find her parents' faces in her own, but sees them in the one-year-old's.

*

"Mama," the thirty-eight-year-old says, pointing at the one-year-old, "Mama."

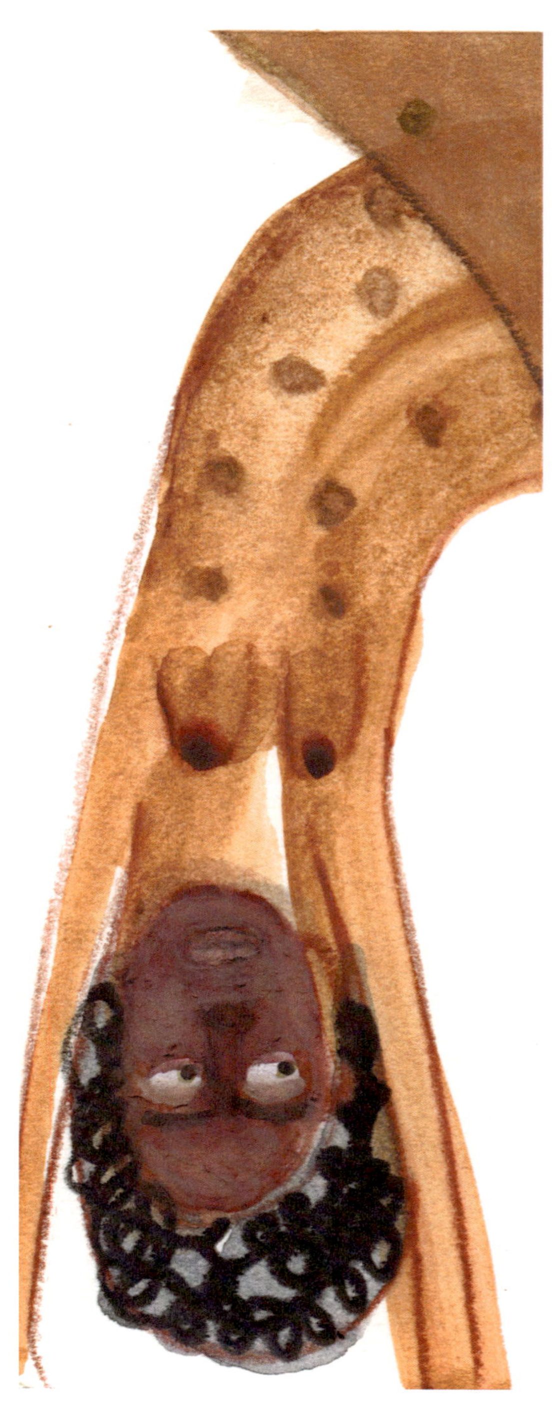

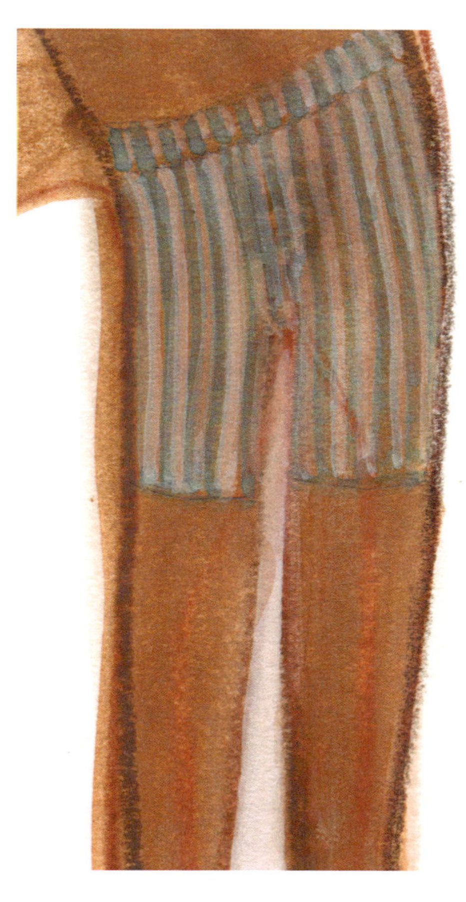

For Something Real

Shana L. Redmond

It has not been at my front of mind but, if I'm honest, I've been thinking a lot about bending. I've not consciously known it as such. My terse tongue has instead framed the anguish and fatigue of this long moment with another bodily analogy: metabolism. Minoritized women have been trained to metabolize pain, to become more efficient in its absorption and redistribution so as to withstand more and more and more, to dole out our fair share of more and more at every level of human interaction in the ever-onward march of racial capitalism: widgets and wars, six-foot fences and settler-colonial occupation. Forget the isolation, toxicity, and the debt—not to one another for the worlds we've heroically labored to create but the debt like a foregrounded charcoal watercolor that has laid waste to our bright horizons.

Yes, metabolism, but bend works too. The expectation being that, in the perpetual stretch and pull against our distinct, thoughtful ways of life and common dignity, our bodies will become more malleable, flexible such that the break (a la, "bend but don't break") will be many years, even decades later. Much like metabolism, we're attempting to delay an inevitable rupture or consumption by the inertia of the world. We might almost be convinced of that possibility if we disregard the empire steadied on backs so disfigured by pressure that upright, upstanding has become a long ago tale, the moral of which we no longer believe. The fractures, herniation, and slippages somehow become tolerable, managed through an elaborate system of forgetting and excusing and stores of fortitude that might otherwise be dedicated to breaking that which breaks us.

Ali's *Studies* series is a redirection that reveals something else. I can't look at the image without being pulled into its mirror. The arc of their hips is a rainbow in reach of something before or below, all the while looking up and forward. It's a call and beckoning desirous of being and knowing against the gravity of harm. What can we see from another vantage—that which we emphatically choose and lay claim to? Arms reaching overhead toward some core or some sky or someone worth the change in direction. Following the gaze of the curly-haired and bent figure, I'm captured by the way they make it look easy, preferable even, staring back at me with acknowledgement. *Your body, your moves,* they seem to say. *Bend for your purposes, your pleasure.* I admire that naked will to reach for something real in antagonism to those who watch in admonishment instead of merited awe. There are wonders every day, after all, not the least of which are our bodies.

Drawing Details
Laylah Ali

Drawings by Laylah Ali

Each work:
Untitled from *Studies* series, 2010-13
Mixed media on card
5 x 3.25 inches or 3 x 4.5 inches

All images © 2024, Laylah Ali

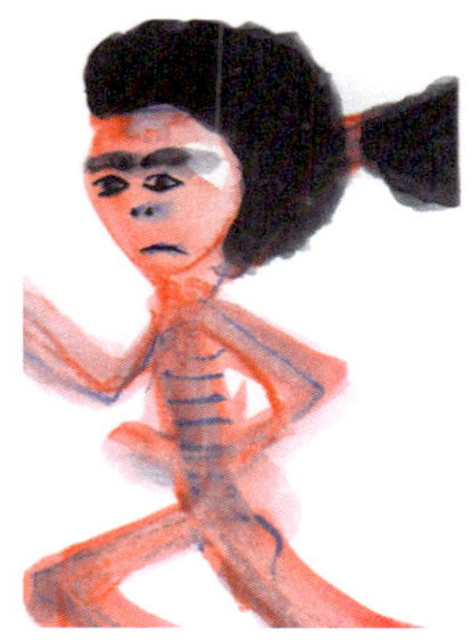
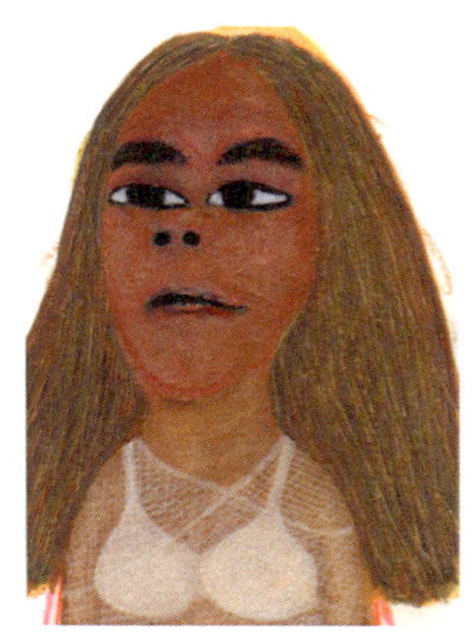
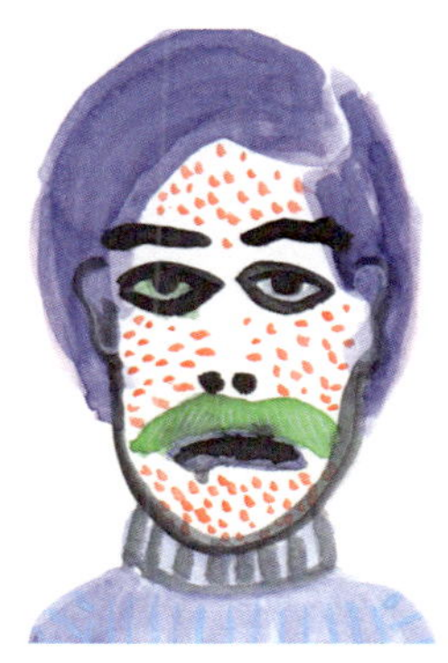
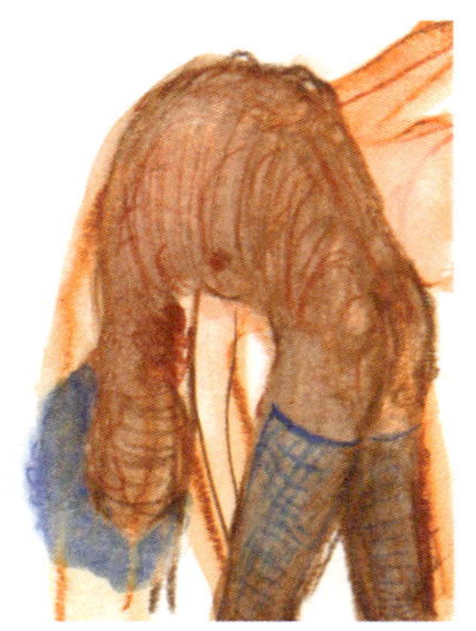
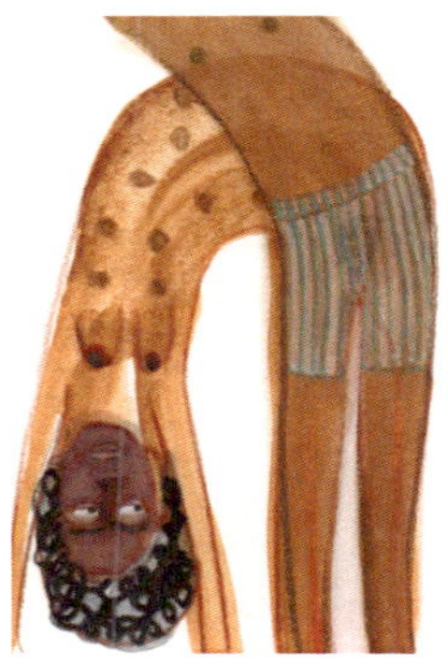
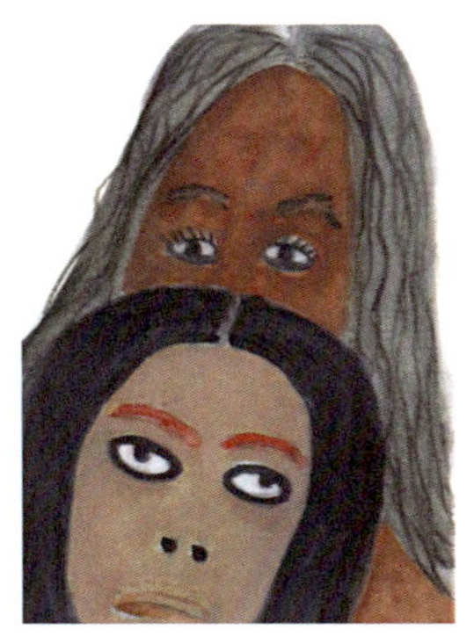

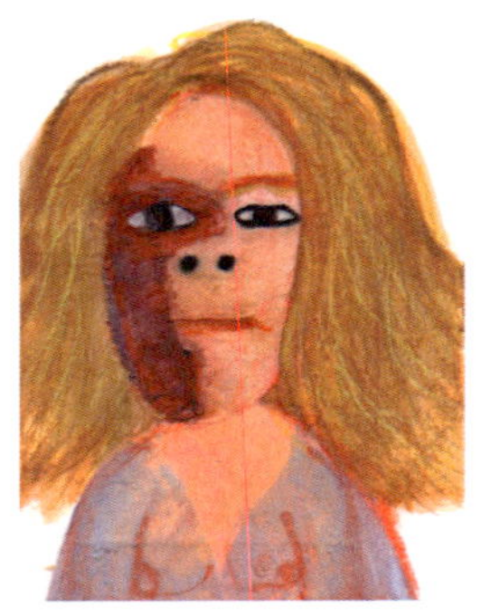
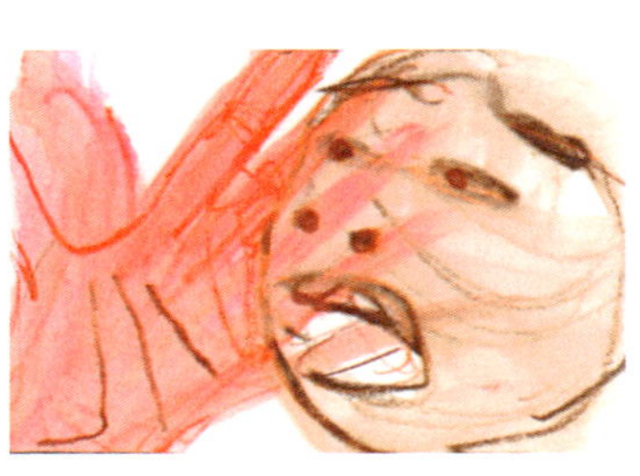
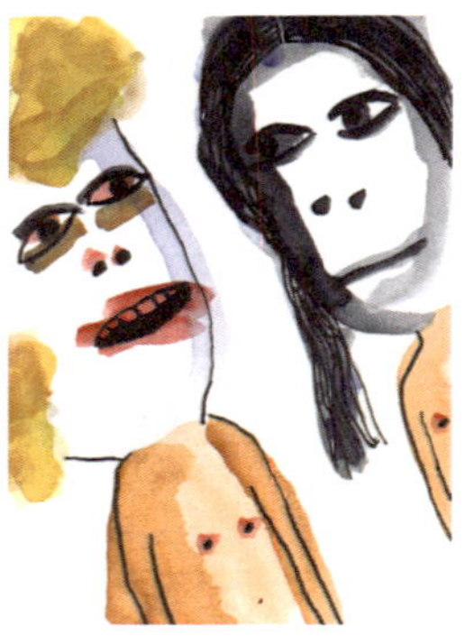
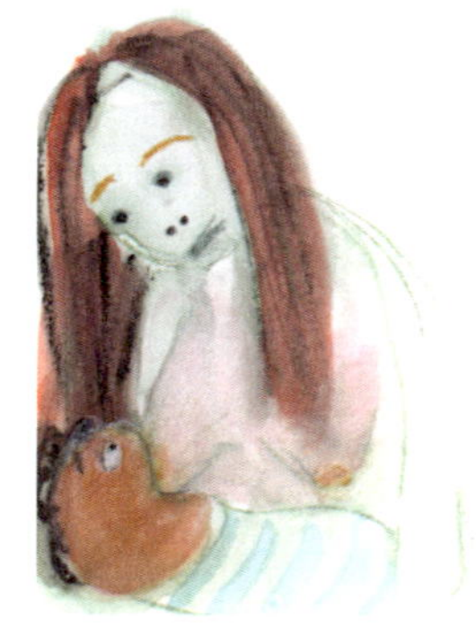
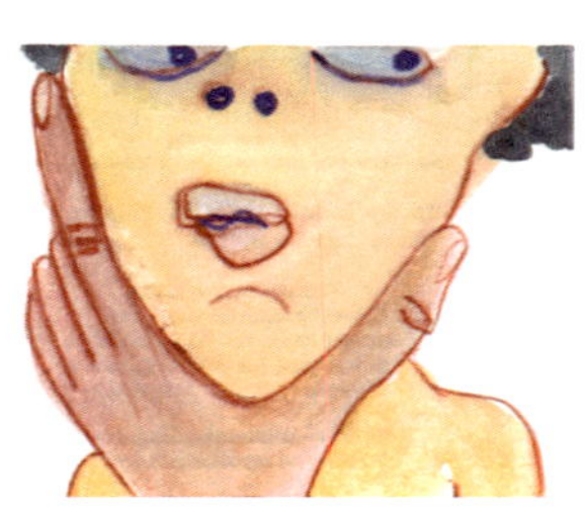
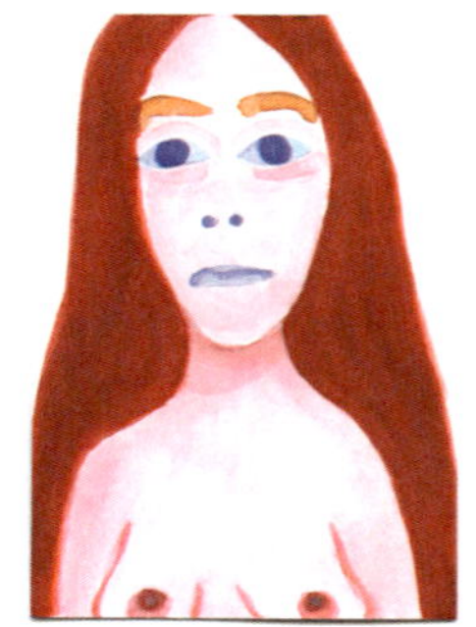

Contributor Bios

Laylah Ali (b. 1968, Buffalo, New York) is an artist based in western Massachusetts. Her latest solo exhibit *Is anything the matter? Drawings by Laylah Ali* opened in January 2024 at the SUNY Fredonia Cathy and Jesse Marion Art Gallery and will travel in 2025 to the University Museum of Contemporary Art at the University of Massachusetts Amherst and Colby College Museum in Maine. Ali has had solo exhibitions at the Museum of Modern Art, New York; Institute of Contemporary Art, Boston; Museum of Contemporary Art Chicago; Contemporary Art Museum, St. Louis; and MASS MoCA, North Adams, Massachusetts, among others, and her work has been exhibited at the Venice Biennale and Whitney Biennial. Ali's works are included in the permanent collections of numerous public institutions, including the Albright-Knox Art Gallery, Buffalo, NY; the Museum of Contemporary Art Chicago; the Museum of Modern Art, New York; the Walker Art Center, Minneapolis; and the Seattle Art Museum. Ali has been the recipient of multiple honors including the Joan Mitchell Foundation Painters and Sculptors Grant, United States Artists Fellowship, William H. Johnson Prize, and the Institute of Contemporary Art Boston Artist Prize. Her work and process were highlighted in season 3 of the acclaimed PBS *Art21* series. She is currently the Francis Christopher Oakley Third Century Professor of Art at Williams College, Williamstown, MA.

Victoria Chang's forthcoming book of poems, *With My Back to the World* will be published in 2024 by Farrar, Straus & Giroux. She is the Bourne Chair in Poetry at Georgia Tech and Director of Poetry@Tech.

Angie Cruz's most recent novel *How Not To Drown in A Glass of Water* (2022) is a finalist for the 2024 Neustadt International Prize for Literature and shortlisted for The Aspen Words Literary Prize. Her novel *Dominicana* (2019) was shortlisted for The Women's Prize, longlisted for the Andrew Carnegie Medals for Excellence in Fiction. She's the founder and Editor-in-Chief of *Aster(ix) Journal* and is currently an Associate Professor at University of Pittsburgh.

A writer of Uruguayan origins, **Caro De Robertis** is the author of six novels, including the forthcoming *The Palace of Eros*; *The President and the Frog*, a finalist for the PEN/Faulkner Award and the PEN/Jean Stein Book Award; and Cantoras, winner of a Stonewall Book Award. Their books have been translated into seventeen languages and have received numerous other honors, including a fellowship from the National Endowment for the Arts and the John Dos Passos Prize. De Robertis is also an award-winning translator of Latin American literature, and a professor at San Francisco State University. They live in Oakland, California with their two children.

Julián Delgado Lopera is the author of The New York Times acclaimed novel Fiebre Tropical (Feminist Press 2020), the Winner of the 2021 Ferro Grumley Award and a 2021 Lambda Literary award; a finalist of the 2020 Kirkus Prize in Fiction and the 2021 Aspen Literary Prize. Julián is also the author of *¡Cuéntamelo!* (Aunt Lute 2017), an illustrated bilingual collection of oral histories by LGBT Latinx immigrants. Julián's received fellowships and residencies from The National Endowment for the Arts, Black Mountain Institute, Creative Work Fund, Hedgebrook,

California Arts Council, San Francisco Arts Commission, Headlands Center for The Arts. Their work has appeared in Granta, Teen Vogue, The Kenyon Review, McSweeney's, The Rumpus, The White Review, LALT, Four Way Review, TimeOut Mag to name a few. They are the former executive director of RADAR Productions and one of the founders of Drag Queen Story Hour. Born and raised in Bogotá, Colombia, Julián currently resides in San Francisco.

Jaquira Díaz is the author of *Ordinary Girls*, winner of a Whiting Award, a Florida Book Awards Gold Medal, a Lambda Literary Awards finalist, an American Booksellers Association Indies Introduce Selection, an Indie Next Pick, a Barnes & Noble Discover Great New Writers Selection, and finalist for the Discover Prize. Díaz has written for *The Atlantic, The Guardian, T: The New York Times Style Magazine,* and elsewhere. Her debut novel, *I Am Deliberate*, is forthcoming from Algonquin Books. She teaches at Columbia University.

Patricia Engel is the author of five works of fiction, including *The Faraway World* (2023) and *Infinite Country* (2021), both published by Avid Reader Press under Simon & Schuster. Born to Colombian parents and raised in New Jersey, Patricia is a graduate of New York University and earned her MFA at Florida International University. She is a Professor of English in the Creative Writing Program at the University of Miami.

Courtney Faye Taylor is a writer, visual artist, and the author of *Concentrate* (Graywolf Press, 2022). The collection was awarded the T.S. Eliot Four Quartets Prize, the Hurston/Wright Legacy Award, the Cave Canem Poetry Prize and was named a finalist for the NAACP Image Awards, the Lambda Literary Awards, and other honors. Courtney lives in Atlanta, Georgia.

Nimmi Gowrinathan is a Tamil Sri-Lankan activist-scholar. She is a Professor at the City College of New York, where she founded the *Politics of Sexual Violence Initiative*, a global initiative that draws on in-depth research to inform movement-building around the impact of sexual violence on women's political identities. As a key part of this initiative she created *Beyond Identity: A Gendered Platform for Scholar-Activists*, a program that seeks to train immigrants and students of color in identity-driven research, political writing, and activism anchored in a thoughtful analysis of structural violence. She provides expert analysis for CNN, MSNBC, AL Jazeera, and the BBC and her writing on gender and violence has been published in *Harper's Magazine, Freeman's Journal, Foreign Affairs*, and *Guernica Magazine* among others. She is the creator of the Female Fighter Series at Guernica Magazine and the Publisher of *Adi Magazine,* a new literary journal to rehumanize policy. Her recent book, *Radicalizing Her,* examines the complex politics of the female fighter (Beacon 2021).

A poet and multimedia artist, **Diana Khoi Nguyen** is the author of *Root Fractures* (2024) and *Ghost Of* (2018), which was a finalist for the National Book Award. Her video work has been exhibited at the Miller ICA. Nguyen is a MacDowell and Kundiman fellow, and a member of the Vietnamese artist collective, She Who Has No Master(s). She's received an NEA fellowship and awards from the 92Y "Discovery" Poetry and 2019 Kate Tufts Discovery contests. She teaches in the Randolph College Low-Residency MFA and is an Assistant Professor at the University of Pittsburgh.

Born and raised in Port Harcourt, Nigeria, **Chinelo Okparanta** received her BS from Pennsylvania State University, her MA from Rutgers University, and her MFA from the Iowa Writers' Workshop. She is the author of *Happiness, Like Water* (2013); *Under the Udala*

Trees (2015); and *Harry Sylvester Bird* (2022). She is a winner of a 2014 Lambda Literary Award, a 2016 Lambda Literary Award, the 2016 Jessie Redmon Fauset Book Award in Fiction, the 2016 Inaugural Betty Berzon Emerging Writer Award from the Publishing Triangle, and a 2014 O. Henry Prize.

A boundaryless writer and scholar, **Shana L. Redmond** (she/her) is the author of *Anthem: Social Movements and the Sound of Solidarity in the African Diaspora* (NYU Press, 2014) and the award-winning *Everything Man: The Form and Function of Paul Robeson* (Duke UP, 2020). She is a 2023 Guggenheim Fellow and professor of English and Comparative Literature and the Center for the Study of Ethnicity and Race at Columbia University.

Lilliam Rivera is a MacDowell fellow and an award-winning author of eight works of fiction: four young adult novels, three middle grade books, and a graphic novel for DC Comics. Her books have been awarded a Pura Belpré Honor, been featured on NPR, *New Yorker, Los Angeles Times, NY Times,* and multiple "best of" lists. Her novel *Never Look Back* is slated for an Amazon movie adaptation. Her writing has appeared in the *Washington Post*, the *New York Times*, and *Elle*, to name a few. Her adult debut *Tiny Threads* (Del Rey Books) will be available in bookstores September 24, 2024. A Bronx, New York native, Lilliam currently lives in Los Angeles.

Alejandro Varela (he/him) is based in New York. His work has appeared in the *Boston, Yale*, and *Georgia Reviews, The Point Magazine, Harper's*, and *the Offing*, among other publications. His debut novel, *The Town of Babylon* (Astra House, 2022) was a finalist for the National Book Award. His short story collection, *The People Who Report More Stress* (Astra, 2023), is one of Publishers Weekly's best works of fiction in 2023, a finalist for the International Latino Book Awards, and longlisted for the Aspen Literary Prize. Varela is an editor-at-large of *Apogee Journal,* and he holds a masters in public health from the University of Washington.

More Aster(ix) Anthologies

10th Anniversary Issue, Part II: Fiction & Interviews
Fall/Winter 2023

10th Anniversary Issue, Part I: Poetry & Nonfiction
Spring/Summer 2023

The Tarot Issue
December 2022

Mothers Unearthed
September 2022

Winter Fiction
December 2021

Best of Hot Metal Bridge
April 2021

The Ferrante Project
October 2020

The Poetry Issue
Winter 2020

Inheritance
Summer 2019

(Un)bound [double issue]
Winter 2018/2019

and more!
available for order wherever books are sold

To read more and see other work published by
Aster(ix), please visit **www.asterixjorunal.com**, scan
the QR code, or follow Aster(ix) on Instagram, Twitter,
and Facebook at **@asterixjournal**

9 781942 547228